SAFETY SUPERHEROES

STAYING SAFE ONLINE

THERESA EMMINIZER

PowerKiDS press.

Published in 2024 by The Rosen Publishing Group, Inc.
2544 Clinton Street, Buffalo, NY 14224

First Edition

Editor: Theresa Emminizer
Book Design: Rachel Rising

Photo Credits: Cover, p. 1 Leningradskaya Mariya/Shutterstock.com; pp. 4, 6, 8, 10, 12, 14, 16, 18, 20 anndypit/Shutterstock.com; p. 5 Dmytro Zinkevych/Shutterstock.com; p. 7 VGstockstudio/Shutterstock.com; p. 9 AnotherPerfectDay/Shutterstock.com; p. 11 Africa Studio/Shutterstock.com; pp. 13, 17, 21 Prostock-studio/Shutterstock.com; p. 15 carballo/Shutterstock.com; p. 19 pathdoc/Shutterstock.com.

Library of Congress Cataloging-in-Publication Data

Names: Emminizer, Theresa.
Title: Staying safe online / Theresa Emminizer.
Description: New York : Powerkids Press, 2024. | Series: Safety superheroes | Includes glossary and index.
Identifiers: ISBN 9781642825961 (pbk.) | ISBN 9781642825978 (library bound) | ISBN 9781642825985 (ebook)
Subjects: LCSH: Internet and children–Juvenile literature. | Internet–Safety measures–Juvenile literature. | Online social networks–Safety measures–Juvenile literature.
Classification: LCC HQ784.I58 E46 2024 | DDC 004.67'8083–dc23

Manufactured in the United States of America

CPSIA Compliance Information: Batch #CSPK24. For Further Information contact Rosen Publishing, at 1-800-237-9932.

CONTENTS

Stay Safe!

The internet is a great tool for learning, talking, and having fun! It's also a very big space that's shared with lots of different people. When you're online, it's important to follow safety rules. Find out how you can be a safety superhero online!

Posting Pictures

Posting means putting something online. Once something is posted online, it's hard to keep **private**. Nobody should ever post pictures of you online without asking your **permission** or your parent's permission first. Not even grownup family members or teachers!

Family Rules

Do you use a phone, tablet, or computer? Many families have rules about how and when kids can use these things. Your family's rules may be different from a friend's. Follow your own family rules, no matter what other kids are doing.

Don't Talk to Strangers

Strangers are people you don't know. Never talk to strangers online! Even if they say they're a kid. If a stranger sends you a message, tell an adult right away. Never share information with someone you meet online. Never agree to meet them in person.

Personal Information

Personal information is information about who you are, where you live, and how to **contact** you. Never share this information online. If an app or site asks for your name, age, or other information to sign in, ask an adult for help.

Keep Passwords Private

Sometimes you need to use a password to sign into a phone, computer, tablet, or site. Never share your passwords with friends or anyone else besides your parents. Someone could use your password to pretend to be you online! They could share your information.

Bullies Online

Bullies are people who say and do mean things or pick on others. Sometimes bullies are people you know from school or real life. Sometimes they're strangers. If someone is bullying you online, don't **respond** to them. Tell an adult you trust.

Use Safe Sites

Only use safe sites that are meant for kids your age. Most **social media** sites are for older kids. Never lie about your age to get into a site or make an account without your parents' permission. Don't click on any links that pop up.

You're a Safety Superhero!

If you ever feel uncomfortable about something you saw online, tell an adult you trust! Even if you broke the rules or clicked on something you shouldn't have. Tell someone. Don't be afraid of getting into trouble. Your safety is more important than anything else.

GLOSSARY

contact: To talk to, call, text, or meet.

permission: Saying something is okay.

private: Kept to yourself or people you trust.

respond: Talk or write back.

social media: Sites or apps like Facebook, Twitter, and Instagram used to share information and pictures.

FOR MORE INFORMATION

BOOKS

Morlock, Rachael. *I Am a Good Digital Citizen: I Am Alert Online*. New York, NY: PowerKids Press, 2020.

Morlock, Rachael. *I Am a Good Digital Citizen: I Am Smart Online*. New York, NY: PowerKids Press, 2020.

WEBSITES

Fun Kids
www.funkidslive.com/learn/top-10-facts/top-10-facts-about-internet-safety/
Follow these steps to stay safe online!

Kids Health
kidshealth.org/en/kids/online-id.html
Learn about your online identity and how to stay safe online.

INDEX